RALEIGH TRAVEL GUIDE

# Exploring Raleigh The Capital City Of North Carolina

by Sheffield's Travel

# CONTENT

Chapter One

Raleigh

II. Practical Information

A. Visas and Entry Requirements

B. Currency and Budgeting

C. Transportation

D. Climate and Best Time to Visit

Chapter Two

III. Accommodations

A. Types of Accommodations

B. Recommendations by Location

 C. Tips for Booking

Chapter Three

IV. Food and Drinks

A. Cuisine Overview

B. Recommendations by Location

C. Eating Out vs. Cooking In

D. Food and Drink Etiquette


Chapter Four

V. Sights and Activities

A. Overview of Attractions

B. Recommendations by Location

C. Outdoor Activities

D. Cultural and Historical Sites


Chapter Five

VI. Maps

A. Overview of Maps


Chapter Six

VII. Safety Information

A. General Safety Tips

B. Emergency Services and Contacts

C. Health and Safety Concerns

D. Specific Safety Concerns by Location


Chapter Seven

VIII. Itinerary Suggestions

A. Overview of Itinerary Options

B. Suggested Itineraries by Interest



Chapter Eight

IX. Language Phrasebook

A. Overview of the Language

B. Common Phrases for Travelers

C. Pronunciation Guide


Chapter Nine

X. Cultural Insights

A. Overview of Culture

B. Customs and Traditions

C. Local Festivals and Celebrations

D. Respectful Travel Practices


XI. Conclusion

# INTRODUCTION

Welcome to Raleigh, the energetic capital city of North Carolina! This city is a clamoring center point of expressions, culture, history, and innovation that offers something for each kind of explorer. Whether you're a foodie, a set of experiences buff, or an open air swashbuckler, Raleigh has a lot to keep you engaged.

First got comfortable the last part of the 1700s, Raleigh is saturated with history, and guests can investigate the city's past through its various galleries and noteworthy locales. Simultaneously, Raleigh is a cutting edge, ground breaking city, and guests can partake in its numerous mechanical and logical headways.

One of the features of Raleigh is its food scene. The city is known for its "ranch to-table" eateries, where gourmet specialists utilize privately obtained fixings to make delectable dishes. Guests can likewise partake in the city's art bottling works and refineries, which offer a wide assortment of lagers and spirits.

Assuming you're an open air devotee, Raleigh will not frustrate. The city flaunts various stops and green spaces, including Umstead State Park, where guests can climb, bicycle, and fish. Also, assuming you're searching for some metropolitan experience, you can investigate Raleigh's numerous areas, each with its own exceptional character and appeal.

We trust this guide will assist you with finding all that Raleigh brings to the table. From its rich history to its cutting edge conveniences, this city is a genuine jewel of the South. So gather your packs and prepare to investigate Raleigh!

## Chapter One

## Raleigh

Raleigh is the capital city of the territory of North Carolina in the US. It is situated in the focal piece of the state, and is perhaps of the quickest developing city in the country. Raleigh is known for its examination and innovation ventures, as well as its numerous colleges and universities. It is likewise home to a few exhibition halls, parks, and other social attractions, like the North Carolina Historical center of Inherent Sciences, the North Carolina Gallery of Craftsmanship, and the North Carolina State Legislative hall. Moreover, Raleigh is essential for the Exploration Triangle area, which incorporates the urban communities of Durham and House of prayer Slope, and is known for its high centralization of innovation organizations and examination establishments.

## II. Practical Information

### A. Visas and Entry Requirements

You may require a visa to enter Raleigh if you are not a citizen of the United States. The kind of visa you need will depend on the reason you are traveling, such as for business, study, or tourism. You can really look at the U.S. Branch of State's site to see whether you really want a visa, and what kind of visa you really want.

If you are coming from a nation that is a participant in the Visa Waiver Program (VWP), you may need to apply for an Electronic System for Travel Authorization (ESTA) in addition to obtaining a visa. Citizens of participating nations can travel to the United States without a visa for up to 90 days under the ESTA. Check the ESTA website to see if you qualify for the program and to submit an application.

It's critical to keep in mind that entry requirements can change frequently, so it's your responsibility to make sure you have the right paperwork before you go. As a result, the most up-to-date information regarding Raleigh's entry requirements should be obtained from either the airline you intend to use or the U.S. embassy or consulate in your home country.

I hope you find this information useful, and I hope your trip to Raleigh is safe and enjoyable!

### B. Currency and Budgeting

Planning your budget and familiarizing yourself with the local currency are essential when visiting Raleigh, North Carolina. Some suggestions:

Currency: The US dollar (USD) is the currency in use in Raleigh, North Carolina. The majority of banks, currency exchange offices, and airports accept foreign currencies in exchange for USD.

Budget: When compared to other major cities in the United States, Raleigh has a lower cost of living than many others. Notwithstanding, it's as yet really smart to design your spending plan ahead of time. When making a travel budget, keep these costs in mind:

Accommodation: The type of accommodation you choose, the location, and the time of year you visit Raleigh all influence how much it will cost to stay there. A room in a mid-range hotel should cost between $100 and $150 per night on average.

Drinks and meals: There are a lot of great restaurants and bars to choose from in Raleigh's food scene. A pint of beer costs between $5 and $7, and the average cost of a meal at a mid-range restaurant is between $15 and $25 per person.

Transportation: GoRaleigh, Raleigh's public transportation system, has buses and a downtown circulator. A day pass costs $6, while a one-way bus ticket costs $2.25. You also have the option of renting a car, which costs around $30 per day.

Activities: Museums, parks, and outdoor activities are just a few of the many low-cost and free activities in Raleigh. The North Carolina State Capitol, Pullen Park, and the North Carolina Museum of Art are among the most well-liked tourist destinations.

Payment Techniques: Credit cards are accepted by most Raleigh businesses, and the city has numerous ATMs where you can withdraw cash. Always bring some cash with you to use for small purchases and tips.

In general, Raleigh is not too expensive to visit, and with careful planning, you can take advantage of everything the city has to offer without breaking the bank.

## C. Transportation

There are a number of ways to get around Raleigh, the capital of North Carolina, including:

Rental cars: At the Raleigh-Durham International Airport and all over the city, you can rent a car. Hertz, Avis, Enterprise, and Budget are a few of Raleigh's most well-known rental car companies.

Transportation options: GoRaleigh, Raleigh's bus system, provides numerous bus routes throughout the city. Additionally, the Raleigh Union Station is a train station in the city that serves various Amtrak destinations.

Services like ride-hailing: In Raleigh, popular ride-hailing services like Uber and Lyft can be used to make reservations through their mobile apps.

Taxis: Additionally, there are taxis all over the city. Raleigh Taxi Service and Yellow Cab of Raleigh are two well-known Raleigh taxi companies.

Walking and bicycling: Raleigh has a network of bike lanes and streets that are friendly to pedestrians, making it simple to walk or ride a bike around the city. The Raleigh-Durham International Airport is one of the city's many locations where you can rent a bike.

Airports:  Raleigh-Durham International Airport (RDU) is the primary airport in Raleigh, North Carolina. It serves the Research Triangle area, which includes Raleigh, Durham, and Chapel Hill. It is about 10 miles northwest of downtown Raleigh. American Airlines and Delta Air Lines use RDU as a hub to fly to a variety of domestic and international destinations, including Europe, Central America, and the Caribbean.

In general, Raleigh offers a wide variety of transportation options, and visitors can easily navigate the city using any of the aforementioned options.

## D. Climate and Best Time to Visit

The climate in Raleigh, North Carolina, the state capital, is humid subtropical with four distinct seasons. While the winters are mild and cool, the summers are hot and humid. The best opportunity to visit Raleigh relies upon your own inclinations and what you believe should do while you're there.

The best times to visit Raleigh are typically from March to May and September to November. During these periods, the weather conditions is gentle, and the city is less packed than throughout the late spring months. Spring is a wonderful chance to visit Raleigh when the blossoms are in sprout, and the city wakes up with celebrations and occasions.

The best time to visit is during the summer, from June to August, if you like warm weather and outdoor activities. However, be prepared for high humidity and temperatures that can make it uncomfortable to spend a lot of time outside.

Due to the possibility of cold and wet weather, the winter months of December through February are typically the least favorable times to visit Raleigh. However, the nearby mountains provide excellent opportunities for skiing and snowboarding if you enjoy winter sports.

In general, the best time to visit Raleigh depends on what you like and want to do there.

# Chapter Two

## III. Accommodations

Where to stay in Raleigh

Raleigh is a popular tourist destination and the state capital of North Carolina. There are a variety of lodging options for visitors to Raleigh that can meet their requirements and budget. Downtown Raleigh, North Hills, and the Research Triangle Park area are some popular places to stay in Raleigh.

In Raleigh, there are numerous hotels, motels, inns, and bed and breakfasts. Guests can likewise track down get-away rentals, like lofts, condominiums, and homes, through sites like Airbnb and VRBO. In addition, visitors who need to remain in Raleigh for an extended period of time can choose from a wide variety of extended-stay accommodations, such as corporate apartments and suites.

## A. Types of Accommodations

Accommodation Options in Raleigh:

Hotels: There are many hotels in Raleigh, from budget-friendly options to luxurious ones. Marriott, Hilton, and Hyatt are a few of Raleigh's most well-known hotel chains.

Motels: For travelers seeking basic lodging, motels are a more cost-effective option. Motel 6 and Super 8 are two of Raleigh's most well-liked hotels.

Overnight boardinghouses: For those who prefer to stay in a home-like setting, bed and breakfasts provide a more intimate setting. The Oakwood Inn and the Arrowhead Inn are two popular Raleigh bed and breakfasts.

Apartments for Rent: Websites like Airbnb and VRBO offer a variety of vacation rentals, including homes, condos, and apartments. In addition to offering more space and amenities than hotels, these rentals frequently come at a lower cost.

Options for Staying Longer: Corporate apartments and suites offer more space and amenities than traditional hotels for visitors who need to stay in Raleigh for a longer period of time. The Staybridge Suites and the Residence Inn are two well-known Raleigh options for extended stays.

## B. Recommendations by Location

Accommodations in Raleigh suggested by location:

When it comes to finding a place to stay, Raleigh is a bustling city with many distinct neighborhoods and areas to choose from. Based on where you are, here are some suggestions:

Raleigh's Downtown: If you stay in the city's center, you'll be close to everything. The Raleigh Convention Center and the North Carolina State Capitol are two of the city's most well-known tourist attractions. The area also has a lot of shops, bars, and restaurants to choose from. Some extraordinary lodging choices in midtown Raleigh incorporate the Raleigh Marriott Downtown area, the Sheraton Raleigh Inn, and the Home Hotel Raleigh Downtown.

Raleigh North: North Raleigh might be a good option for you if you want a quieter, more suburban lifestyle. Beautiful parks, green spaces, and high-end shopping malls are common in this area. The Residence Inn Raleigh Midtown, the Hyatt Place Raleigh-North, and the Renaissance Raleigh North Hills Hotel are all excellent options for lodging in North Raleigh.

Park Research Triangle: Staying close to the Research Triangle Park might be a good option if you're traveling to Raleigh for business. Many of the city's largest businesses and research institutions are located in this area. The Courtyard by Marriott Raleigh-Durham Airport/Morrisville, the Hilton Garden Inn Raleigh-Durham/Research Triangle Park, and the Staybridge Suites Raleigh-Durham Airport are a few of the hotels in the Research Triangle Park vicinity.

## C. Tips for Booking

Advice for Finding a Place to Stay in Raleigh:

Plan ahead: Raleigh is a popular place to go, especially during the busiest times for travel. Make your reservation for a place to stay as soon as you can to guarantee both the best price and availability.

Think about the location: Choose your Raleigh lodging in accordance with your desired location. Look for hotels in that area if you want to be close to downtown and all the action. North Raleigh is a good option if you want a more suburban, tranquil setting.

Examine reviews: Read reviews left by other travelers before making a reservation for your lodging. This can help you avoid unpleasant surprises and give you an idea of what to expect.

Find bargains: Watch out for arrangements and limits, particularly in the event that you're going during the slow time of year. If you make your reservation at the right time, you might be able to cut costs on your lodging.

Think about other choices: Raleigh has many unique lodging options, including vacation rentals, bed and breakfasts, and hotels. If you're looking for a one-of-a-kind, memorable experience, think about these other options.

# Chapter Three

## IV. Food and Drinks

Raleigh, North Carolina's capital, has a thriving food and drink scene that caters to all tastes and budgets. The following are some of Raleigh's most popular dining and drinking options:

BBQ: Clyde Cooper's BBQ, The Pit Authentic BBQ, and Ole Time Barbecue are just a few of the Raleigh establishments that offer mouthwatering barbecue.

Southern food: In Raleigh, you can also find traditional Southern fare like collard greens, biscuits, and fried chicken. Beasley's Chicken + Honey, Poole's Diner, and Dame's Chicken and Waffles are a few popular options.

Craft brews: Raleigh has a flourishing specialty lager scene, and there are numerous distilleries and pubs where you can test neighborhood mixes. Raleigh Brewing Company, Trophy Brewing Company, and Bond Brothers Beer Company are a few well-known choices.

Coffee: Raleigh has many choices for coffee lovers, including local establishments like Jubala Coffee and Sola Coffee Cafe.

Seafood: There are a number of seafood restaurants in Raleigh, including 42nd Street Oyster Bar and The Cortez Seafood + Cocktail, if you're craving seafood.

Dishes from other cultures: Mexican, Indian, Italian, and Thai are just a few of the many international cuisine options available in Raleigh. A few famous spots to attempt incorporate Guasaca, Biryani Maxx, and Farina Area Italian.

In general, Raleigh's food and beverage scene has something for everyone.

## A. Cuisine Overview

A Review of Raleigh's Cuisine:

The food scene in Raleigh, North Carolina, is diverse and offers a variety of options, including seafood, barbecue, Southern cuisine, and international cuisines like Italian, Mexican, and Asian. Sweet potato pie, Carolina-style barbecue, and biscuits and gravy are among the region's most well-liked dishes. There are also a lot of local coffee shops and a growing craft beer scene in the city.

Nearby regulations with respect to the utilization of liquor, including not driving under the influence.

## B. Recommendations by Location

Location-Based Recommendations:

Beasley's Chicken + Honey in Raleigh's downtown offers Southern-style cuisine. Try the Raleigh Times Bar in the Warehouse District for seafood. For Italian, look at Sauce in the Moore Square locale. Brewery Bhavana in the downtown area serves Asian fare. In the Glenwood South area, Centro serves Mexican fare. The Pit Authentic BBQ, Bida Manda Laotian Restaurant and Bar, and Sitti Authentic Lebanese are all popular Raleigh eateries.

## C. Eating Out vs. Cooking In

Dining Out versus Home Cooking:

In Raleigh, personal preferences and circumstances determine whether to cook or eat out. While cooking at home can be more cost-effective and allow for greater control over the ingredients, dining out can be a great way to explore the city's food scene and try new dishes. Cooking at home can also be a good option for people who want to eat healthier or have dietary restrictions. Whole Foods Market, Trader Joe's, and Harris Teeter are among Raleigh's most well-known grocery stores.

## D. Food and Drink Etiquette

Manner with Food and Drink:

At restaurants, it is common practice in Raleigh to leave a 15-20% tip. It is also essential to be aware of any particular dining traditions associated with distinct cuisines, such as not asking for Parmesan cheese with seafood pasta in an Italian restaurant or removing one's shoes before entering a Japanese restaurant. Furthermore, it's essential to know about.

# Chapter Four

## V. Sights and Activities

Raleigh, North Carolina's capital, is well-known for its beautiful parks, vibrant arts and culture scene, and rich history. Consider these popular tourist attractions and activities:

The North Carolina Museum of Natural Sciences is worth a visit. Dinosaurs, live animals, and an impressive collection of minerals and gems are just some of the exhibits and interactive displays this museum has to offer.

Take in the sights at the North Carolina Museum of Art: Contemporary art, African art, and European paintings are just a few of the many types of art on display in this museum's collection from a variety of periods.

Take a look at the old State Capitol building: This historic building, which has served as the seat of North Carolina's government since 1840, is open to the public for guided tours.

Take a stroll through the JC Raulston Arboretum's stunning gardens: There are many unusual and rare species of plants in this botanical garden's diverse collection.

At Umstead State Park, you can do the following things outside: This park offers climbing, trekking, fishing, and setting up camp open doors in a beautiful regular setting.

Visit the North Carolina State Fair: This beloved local tradition, which takes place every October, has carnival rides, food vendors, and agricultural exhibits.

Get a show at the Duke Energy Place for the Performing Expressions: Concerts, dance performances, and Broadway shows are just some of the performances that take place here.

Take a look at the State Farmers Market in North Carolina: Fresh produce, flowers, and handmade crafts from local vendors can be found at this bustling market.

Visit the historic Oakwood neighborhood on foot: Numerous 19th-century historic homes can be found in this neighborhood, which is popular for walking tours.

Take in the local dining scene: There are a lot of restaurants in Raleigh that serve seafood, international cuisine, and Southern cuisine. Don't miss out on the famous barbecue from North Carolina!

## A. Overview of Attractions

A Brief Description of Raleigh's Attractions:

Raleigh, North Carolina's capital, offers a wide range of attractions to suit a variety of interests. Raleigh's most popular attractions include:

Museum of Natural Sciences in North Carolina: This well-known museum has science and natural history exhibits.

North Carolina Historical center of Workmanship: This historical center highlights a great many craftsmanship from various periods and styles, including contemporary workmanship.

Park Pullen: There is a carousel, train ride, and paddle boats at this popular family-friendly park.

The Old Oakwood: The homes in this Raleigh neighborhood, which dates back to the Victorian era, are in excellent condition.

Marbles Museum for Kids: Exhibits on science, technology, engineering, and math (STEM) topics make this a fun, hands-on museum for kids.

## B. Recommendations by Location

Location-Based Recommendations:

Raleigh's Downtown: The North Carolina Museum of Art and the North Carolina Museum of Natural Sciences are two of the many attractions in the lively Downtown Raleigh area. Downtown is also home to the State Capitol, where visitors can take a guided tour to learn about the building's history and the history of the state.

The Old Oakwood: Architecture enthusiasts must visit this historic neighborhood. The well-preserved Victorian homes can be admired on a self-guided walking tour.

West Glenwood: There are many bars, restaurants, and clubs in this area, which is known for its nightlife. Additionally, the Contemporary Art Museum, which features rotating modern art exhibits, is open to visitors.

Park Pullen: This park is a great option for families with young children because it is close to the campus of North Carolina State University. The park has a playground and picnic areas in addition to the paddle boats, train ride, and carousel.

## C. Outdoor Activities

Outdoor Recreation:

State Park William B. Umstead: Over 5,500 acres of natural beauty can be found in this park, which is just outside of Raleigh. On the park's numerous trails, visitors can hike, bike, or ride horses. They can also fish or boat on one of the park's lakes.

The Neuse River Trail Walking, running, or cycling on this 27-mile paved trail is ideal. It winds along the Neuse River, giving you a chance to see local wildlife and beautiful views.

Lake Johnson Park: The large lake in this park in southwest Raleigh is ideal for kayaking, fishing, or simply unwinding by the water. The recreation area additionally has climbing and trekking trails, as well as cookout regions.

State Recreation Area Jordan Lake: This park has a large lake with swimming, boating, and fishing opportunities. It is about 30 minutes from Raleigh. Camping sites and hiking trails are also available in the park.

## D. Cultural and Historical Sites

Raleigh, the capital city of North Carolina, is home to a few social and verifiable locales that feature the district's rich history and legacy. Here are probably the main social and verifiable destinations in Raleigh:

### North Carolina Exhibition hall of History: This historical center grandstands the historical backdrop of North Carolina, from pre-pilgrim times to the current day. It has shows on Local American societies, the Progressive Conflict, the Nationwide conflict, and the state's part in the twentieth hundred years.

**North Carolina State Legislative center:** Finished in 1840, the North Carolina State house is one of the best instances of Greek Restoration design in the country. It filled in as the state's legislative center until 1963 and is presently a Public Memorable Milestone.

**Memorable Oakwood Burial ground:** This graveyard is the last resting spot of large numbers of Raleigh's most unmistakable residents, including lead representatives, congresspersons, and other eminent figures. It additionally has a few delightful tombs and landmarks.

**City Market:** Situated in midtown Raleigh, City Market is a memorable shopping locale that traces all the way back to the mid 1900s. It has a few remarkable shops and eateries, including a fish market that has been doing business for more than 75 years.

**Joel Path Historical center House:** Worked in 1769, the Joel Path Gallery House is perhaps of the most seasoned house in Raleigh. It was the home of Joel Path, a conspicuous figure in North Carolina's initial history, and presently fills in as an exhibition hall committed to his life and times.

**African American Social Complex:** This historical center features the set of experiences and commitments of African Americans in North Carolina. It has shows on subjection, the social equality development, and the accomplishments of noticeable African Americans from the state.

**Yates Plant:** This reestablished eighteenth century gristmill is situated in a picturesque park in Raleigh and is one of only a handful of exceptional leftover water-fueled factories nearby. Guests can visit the factory and find out about its set of experiences and activity.

These are only a couple of the numerous social and verifiable destinations in Raleigh. Whether you are a set of experiences buff or just keen on studying the region, there is a lot to see and investigate in the city.

Chapter Five

VI. Maps

A. Overview of Maps

There are different kinds of guides that can be utilized for Raleigh, North Carolina, contingent upon the reason and setting of the guide. Some examples include:

Road map : Raleigh's major highways, streets, and landmarks are depicted on a road map. This kind of map can be used to find your way and get directions.

Map of topography: The area's elevation and terrain features, such as mountains, valleys, and water bodies, are depicted on a Raleigh topographic map. Hikers, bikers, and other outdoor enthusiasts will find this kind of map useful.

Map of politics: The city, county, and state boundaries, as well as the locations of schools, government buildings, and other civic institutions, are depicted on a political map of Raleigh.

Map for tourism: The most popular Raleigh attractions, restaurants, and entertainment options are highlighted on a tourist map. Visitors who want to learn more about the area can use this kind of map.

Map of public transportation: The local bus and train systems' routes and stops are depicted on a Raleigh transit map. Travelers and commuters who need to use public transportation to get around the city can benefit from this kind of map.

Drafting map: The various land use zones in Raleigh, including residential, commercial, and industrial areas, are depicted on a zoning map. This sort of guide is helpful for engineers and realtors who need to grasp the drafting guidelines nearby.

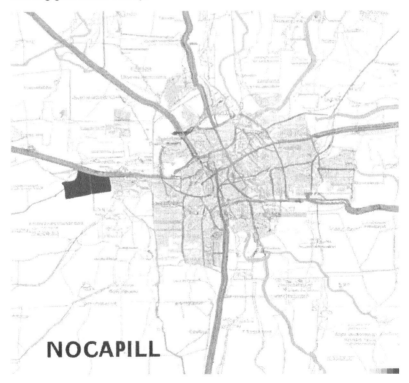

# Chapter Six

## VII. Safety Information

### A. General Safety Tips

Tips for general safety:

Keep an open mind and be aware of your surroundings, especially when you're in tourist or pedestrian-heavy areas.

Never venture out on your own at night or in dimly lit areas.

Make sure your jewelry, phone, and other valuables are safe and out of sight.

When you park, lock the doors and roll up the windows.

Even if your vehicle is locked, do not leave any valuables inside.

Utilize a taxi, ride-sharing help, or public transportation as opposed to strolling or driving in the event that you're new to the area.

Utilize sound judgment and pay attention to your gut feelings.

### B. Emergency Services and Contacts

Contacts and Emergency Services:

Police, Fire, and Medical Emergency: Dial 911

Non-Emergency Police: (919) 996-3335

Poison Control: (800) 222-1222

## C. Health and Safety Concerns

Safety and Health Issues:

In order to stay safe from the sun and stay hydrated in Raleigh's humid subtropical climate,

Be aware that the area is susceptible to pollen and other allergens if you have allergies.

Ticks can carry Lyme disease, so be careful when you're outside.

During the summer, mosquitoes are common, so if you can, wear long sleeves and pants and use an insect repellent.

## D. Specific Safety Concerns by Location

Localized Specific Safety Concerns:

Raleigh's Downtown: Downtown Raleigh is generally safe, but stay in well-lit areas at night and be cautious. Pay attention to panhandlers and those who might try to ask for money from you.

University of North Carolina State: Because NCSU is a big campus, students should be aware of their surroundings and take precautions to avoid being robbed or attacked.

PNC Field: Concerts and sporting events frequently take place at PNC Arena. When leaving the arena at night, be careful because of the large crowds.

State Park William B. Umstead: When it comes to outdoor activities and hiking, Umstead Park is a popular destination. Stay on marked trails and be wary of ticks and other wildlife.

# Chapter Seven

## VIII. Itinerary Suggestions

### A. Overview of Itinerary Options

An Overview of Possible Routes:

Visitors to Raleigh, North Carolina, can take part in a wide range of activities and sights. There is something for everyone in this region, from its stunning museums and parks to its historic landmarks and mouthwatering cuisine. When planning your trip to Raleigh, consider the following possible itineraries:

City Investigation - investigate the midtown region, visit historical centers and exhibitions, shop at neighborhood stores, and eat at a portion of the city's top cafés.

Outdoor Adventure: Take a day trip to nearby lakes or mountains, or go hiking, biking, or kayaking in one of Raleigh's numerous parks and green spaces.

Visit the State Capitol Building, the Governor's Mansion, and the North Carolina Museum of History, three of the city's historic landmarks.

Food and Drink: Take a food and drink tour of the city to try barbecue and craft beer, two types of local cuisine.

# B. Suggested Itineraries by Interest

Tours Based on Your Interests:

City Sightseeing:

Day 1:

Visit the North Carolina Museum of Art to begin the day, which has over 40 galleries and a 164-acre park with outdoor sculptures.

After lunch at a local restaurant, visit the historic City Market and shop at local galleries and boutiques.

Visit the North Carolina Museum of Natural Sciences in the afternoon, which has interactive exhibits and live animals and is one of the largest natural history museums in the Southeast.

Dinner and drinks at one of the best restaurants in the city, like Poole's Diner or Brewery Bhavana, are a great way to end the day.

Day 2:

Take a historic downtown Raleigh walking tour to begin the day, stopping at landmarks like the Governor's Mansion and the State Capitol Building.

Lunch can be had at one of the city's food halls, like Morgan Street Food Hall or Transfer Co. Food Hall, which has a lot of local vendors.

In the early evening, visit the Contemporary Craftsmanship Gallery Raleigh or the North Carolina Historical center of History.

At a rooftop bar like the Durham Hotel rooftop or the Raleigh Times rooftop, enjoy a cocktail to end the day.

Outdoor Activities:

Day 1:

Start the day with a hike at Umstead State Park, which has scenic lakes and more than 5,500 acres of forest.

Enjoy fishing or kayaking in one of the park's lakes after lunch at the picnic area.

Visit the Raleigh Beer Garden in the afternoon to sample more than 350 beers on tap.

Dinner at a local barbecue joint like Clyde Cooper's or The Pit is a good way to end the day.

Day 2:

Jordan Lake, which is just 30 minutes from Raleigh, is a great place to spend the day boating, swimming, and hiking.

After lunch at the marina on the lake, go to a winery or brewery in the area.

End the day with supper at a fish eatery, like the St. Roch Clam Bar or Local people Shellfish Bar.

Places of Interest:

Day 1:

Visit the 1840 North Carolina State Capitol Building and the North Carolina

Executive Mansion, the governor's residence, to begin the day.

Lunch at a historic establishment, such as The Angus Barn or the 18 Seaboard,

The North Carolina Museum of History has exhibits on the state's history from prehistoric times to the present. Visit in the afternoon.

Dinner at a historic establishment, such as The Chef and the Farmer or The Fearrington House, is a good way to end the day.

Day 2:

Take a day trip to the historic town of New Bern, two hours from Raleigh, where Pepsi was born and features colonial architecture.

Lunch at a neighborhood restaurant.

# Chapter Eight

## IX. Language Phrasebook

### A. Overview of the Language

Outline of the Language:

The essential language spoken in Raleigh is English. The vernacular verbally expressed in Raleigh is like General American English, for certain southern accents present. The language is generally perceived and spoken by the vast majority in the city, remembering those for the assistance business.

### B. Common Phrases for Travelers

Familiar Expressions for Travelers

Hi - Hey/Hi

Farewell - Bye/Farewell

Much obliged to you - Thank you/Thanks

My pleasure - My pleasure/No issue

Excuse me - Excuse me/Excuse me

Do you communicate in English? - Do you communicate in English?

I don't have the foggiest idea - I don't have the foggiest idea

Might you at any point rehash that, please? - Might you at any point rehash that, please?

Where could the bathroom be? - Where could the bathroom be?

What amount does this cost? - What amount does this cost?

## C. Pronunciation Guide

Articulation Guide:

Hello there -/haɪ/

Hi -/hɛˈloʊ/

Bye -/baɪ/

Farewell -/gʊdˈbaɪ/

Much thanks to you -/ˈθæŋk ju/

Much obliged -/θæŋks/

The pleasure is all mine -/jʊr ˈwɛlkəm/

Don't sweat it -/noʊ ˈprɑbləm/

Excuse me -/ɪkˈskjuz mi/

Excuse me -/ˈpɑrdən mi/

Do you communicate in English? -/du ju spiːk ˈɪŋglɪʃ/

I don't have the foggiest idea -/aɪ doʊnt ˌʌndərˈstænd/

Might you at any point rehash that, please? -/kʊd ju rɪˈpiːt ðæt pliːz/

Where could the bathroom be? -/wɛr ɪz ðə ˈrɛstrum/

What amount does this cost? -/haʊ mʌtʃ ˈdʌz ðɪs kɔst/

# Chapter Nine

## X. Cultural Insights

### A. Overview of Culture

Cultural Overview:

Raleigh, North Carolina's capital, has a diverse population, cuisine, and art that reflect its rich cultural heritage. The city has a thriving arts and music scene, combining Southern charm with contemporary style. Additionally, the city is a hub for intellectual pursuits and innovation thanks to its numerous universities and research centers.

### B. Customs and Traditions

Traditions and Customs:

Raleigh, like many Southern cities, has a strong sense of friendliness and hospitality. Locals frequently greet one another warmly and engage in conversation. In addition, the city has a thriving culinary scene, with popular favorites like sweet tea, fried chicken, and barbecue. Additionally, the city has a long history of supporting local musicians and artists, and numerous events and venues showcase the creative community of Raleigh.

### C. Local Festivals and Celebrations

Local Celebrations and Festivals:

Throughout the year, Raleigh puts on a number of festivals and celebrations that show off the city's artistic legacy and diversity of culture. The annual International Festival of Raleigh, which features food, dance, and music from all over the world, is one of the most popular events. The North Carolina State Fair, the Wide Open Bluegrass festival, and the Artsplosure festival are all noteworthy events.

## D. Respectful Travel Practices

### Traveling with Respect

When you go to Raleigh, it's important to follow the traditions and customs of the area. The city's Southern hospitality should be remembered by visitors, and they should have pleasant conversations with the locals. Respect for the city's diverse population and cultural heritage is also essential. To fully appreciate Raleigh's cultural offerings, visitors should sample the local cuisine and attend cultural events. Last but not least, visitors should travel in a sustainable manner and be aware of their impact on the environment.

## XI. Conclusion

In conclusion, Raleigh, North Carolina, is an excellent destination for tourists seeking a blend of modern conveniences and Southern charm. Raleigh has something for everyone, whether you're interested in history, culture, food, or outdoor activities. There are numerous opportunities to discover the region's beauty and diversity, such as touring the downtown museums and galleries or hiking the parks' trails.

Raleigh has established itself as a must-visit destination in the Southeast thanks to its world-class cuisine, vibrant nightlife, and thriving art scene. Raleigh has something for everyone, whether you're a solo traveler, a couple, or a family. Therefore, gather your belongings and get ready to take in the entirety of this charming city!

Printed in Great Britain
by Amazon

24510688R00029